MW00884303

LIVE

IN

ME

JESUS

Uplifting Scriptures King James Version

1

To Macari Thank you for Your Support !! Cornelious

Live In Me Jesus, a book of scriptures that I reference when I'm going through hard times, trials and tribulations. Jesus lives in me as he is my help when I'm in a weary place, he is my comfort when I'm alone and he is the one who I put my trust. The scriptures included in this book are those that I grew up with as a young boy in South Carolina. I heard my Grandmothers, Mother and Aunts speak these scriptures when they needed an uplifting word. My prayer is for these scriptures to uplift the world. Live In Me Jesus is my thank you for God for being who he is..... Jehovah – The Lord;

Adonai Jehovah-The Lord God;

Jehovah Adon Kal Ha'arets –The Lord of All the Earth;

Jehovah Bara – The Lord Creator;

Jehovah Chezeq – The Lord My Strength;

Jehovah Chereb – The Lord, the Sword;

Jehovah Eli – The Lord My God;

Jehovah Elyon – The Lord Most High;

Jehovah 'Ez-Lami – The Lord My Strength;

Jehovah Gador Milchamah – The Lord Mighty in Battle;

Jehovah Ganan – The Lord Our Defense;

Jehovah Go'el – The Lord Thy Redeemer;

Jehovah Hashopet – The Lord the Judge;

Jehovah Hoshe'ah – The Lord Save;

Jehovah 'Immeku – The Lord Is with you;

Jehovah 'Izoz Hakaboth – The Lord Strong and Mighty;

Jehovah Jireh – The Lord will Provide;

Jehovah Kabodhi – The Lord My Glory;

Jehovah Kanna – The Lord Whose Name is Jealous;

Jehovah Keren-Yish'i – The Lord the Horn of My Salvation;

Jehovah Machsi – The Lord My Refuge;

Jehovah Magen – The Lord, the Shield;

Jehovah Ma'oz – The Lord, My Fortress;
JehovahHamelech – The Lord the King;
Jehovah Melech 'Olam – The Lord King Forever;
Jehovah Mephalti – The Lord My Deliverer;
Jehovah M'gaddishcem – The Lord Our Sanctifier;
Jehovah Metsodhathi – The Lord, My Fortress;
Jehovah Misqabbi – The Lord My High Tower;
Jehovah Naheh – The Lord that Smiteth;
Jehovah Nissi – The Lord Our Banner;
Jehovah 'Ori – The Lord My Light;
Jehovah Rapha – The Lord that Healeth;
Jehovah Rohi – The Lord My Shepherd;
Jehovah Saboath – The Lord of Hosts;
Jehovah Sel'i – The Lord My Roc;
Jehovah Shalom – The Lord Our Peace;
Jehovah Shammah – The Lord is There;
Jehovah Tiskenu – The Lord Our Righteousness,
Jehovah Tsori – O Lord My Strength;
Jehovah 'Uzam – The Lord Their Strength;
and Jehovah Yasha – The Lord Thy Saviour.

Table of Content

Jehovah Nissi - The Lord Our Banner

Our God is a Consistent God - trust Him you can rely on Him.

Our God Loves Worship and is the Lord of War - God has promised us that He will never leave us nor forsake us and that be with us even until the end of the age. When we worship God, principalities are destroyed.

Our God is a God of Love - The Lord Our Banner. He is confirming to us that indeed His banner over us is love.

Psalms 20:5 (Banner)

"We will rejoice in thy salvation, and in the name of our God we will set up _our_ banners: the LORD fulfil all thy petitions."

Psalms 60:4 (Banner)

"Thou hast given a banner to them that fear thee, that it may be displayed because of the truth. Selah."

Song of Solomon 2:4 (Banner)

"He brought me to the banqueting house, and his banner over me *was* love."

Isaiah 13:2 (Banner)

"Lift ye up a banner upon the high mountain, exalt the voice unto them, shake the hand, that they may go into the gates of the nobles."

During my trials and tribulations in my life, God has always been there for me. He may not come when I wanted him but he always showed up on time. I had to learn to trust in God, trust in his word, rely on him, give him all the praises, love myself and understand that God loved me.

Jehovah Rapha – The Lord that Healeth

I am The Lord your physician.
I am the Lord your healer.

Isaiah 53:5 (Healing)

"But he _was_ wounded for our transgressions, _he was_ bruised for our iniquities: the chastisement of our peace _was_ upon him; and with his stripes we are healed."

Jeremiah 17:14 (Healing)

"Heal me, O LORD, and I shall be healed; save me, and I shall be saved: for thou _art_ my praise."

Isaiah 41:10 (Healing)

"Fear thou not; for I _am_ with thee: be not dismayed; for I _am_ thy God: I will strengthen thee; yea, I will help thee; yea, I will uphold thee with the right hand of my righteousness."

Jeremiah 33:6 (Healing)

"Behold, I will bring it health and cure, and I will cure them, and will reveal unto them the abundance of peace and truth

James 5:15 (Healing)

"And the prayer of faith shall save the sick, and the Lord shall raise him up; and if he have committed sins, they shall be forgiven him."

James 5:14 (Healing)

"Is any sick among you? let him call for the elders of the church; and let them pray over him, anointing him with oil in the name of the Lord:"

Psalms 103:2 (Healing)

"Bless the LORD, O my soul, and forget not all his benefits:"

Psalms 103:3 (Healing)

"Who forgiveth all thine iniquities; who healeth all thy diseases;"

Psalms 103:4 (Healing)

"Who redeemeth thy life from destruction; who crowneth thee with lovingkindness and tender mercies;"

Mark 11:24 (Healing Power)

"Therefore I say unto you, What things soever ye desire, when ye pray, believe that ye receive *them*, and ye shall have *them*."

James 4:7 (Healing Power)

"Submit yourselves therefore to God. Resist the devil, and he will flee from you."

Hebrews 13:8 (Healing Power)

"Jesus Christ the same yesterday, and to day, and for ever."

Matthew 10:1 (Healing Power)

"And when he had called unto *him* his twelve disciples, he gave them power *against* unclean spirits, to cast them out, and to heal all manner of sickness and all manner of disease."

1 Peter 2:24 (Healing Power)

"Who his own self bare our sins in his own body on the tree, that we, being dead to sins, should live unto righteousness: by whose stripes ye were healed."

Growing up as a child I had unbearable headaches that would last for days. I remember constant crying due to the pain. I would be delirious, mother did all that she could do to help with my headaches by giving me children Bayer aspirin. The headaches occurred until I was nine years old. Mother and her praying sister anointed me with holy oil and continued to pray over me until God healed me of the headaches.

Jehovah Shalom – The Lord Our Peace

Who do you turn to when you are in trouble?

Who do you turn to when you are suffering?

Who do you turn to when you worry?

Who do your turn to when your money is low?

Isaiah 26:3 (Peace)

"Thou wilt keep *him* in perfect peace, *whose* mind *is* stayed *on thee*: because he trusteth in thee."

2 Thessalonians 3:16 (Peace)

"Now the Lord of peace himself give you peace always by all means. The Lord *be* with you all."

Matthew 5:9 (Peace)

"Blessed *are* the peacemakers: for they shall be called the children of God."

Philippians 4:6 (Peace)

"Be careful for nothing; but in every thing by prayer and supplication with thanksgiving let your requests be made known unto God."

John 16:33 (Peace)

"These things I have spoken unto you, that in me ye might have peace. In the world ye shall have tribulation: but be of good cheer; I have overcome the world."

Romans 15:13 (Peace)

"Now the God of hope fill you with all joy and peace in believing, that ye may abound in hope, through the power of the Holy Ghost."

1 Corinthians 14:33 (Peace)

"For God is not *the author* of confusion, but of peace, as in all churches of the saints."

1 Peter 5:6 (Peace)

"Humble yourselves therefore under the mighty hand of God, that he may exalt you in due time:"

1 Peter 5:7 (Peace)

"Casting all your care upon him; for he careth for you."

Isaiah 12:2 (Peace)

"Behold, God *is* my salvation; I will trust, and not be afraid: for the LORD JEHOVAH *is* my strength and *my* song; he also is become my salvation."

When trying to decide if I should leave my current job or remain on the job, I gave it to God. I asked for his guidance regarding what I should do. I went on interviews then the Lord spoke to my spirit. In his words he informed me to be still and wait on him. I was at peace because I knew if he intended for me to leave my current job he would open those doors. The Lord spoke to my spirit by showing me how he has kept me this far; leaving home at the age of 18 for boot Navy Boot Camp training in San Diego, California;, safely traveling the seas doing two six month deployments in the Persian Gulf, having the courage to leave the Navy with an honorable discharge at the end of my enlistments, relocating to Atlanta without a job, enrolling in college completing with my Bachelor Degree and having a job two months before graduation.

Jehovah Tiskenu – The Lord Our Righteousness

Righteousness - doing that which is right.

2 Corinthians 5:21(Righteousness)

"For he hath made him *to be* sin for us, who knew no sin; that we might be made the righteousness of God in him."

1 John 2:29 (Righteousness)

"If ye know that he is righteous, ye know that every one that doeth righteousness is born of him."

Philippians 1:11 (Righteousness)

"Being filled with the fruits of righteousness, which are by Jesus Christ, unto the glory and praise of God."

1 Peter 3:14 (Righteousness)

"But and if ye suffer for righteousness' sake, happy *are ye*: and be not afraid of their terror, neither be troubled;"

1 Peter 5:10 (Righteousness)

"But the God of all grace, who hath called us unto his eternal glory by Christ Jesus, after that ye have suffered a while, make you perfect, stablish, strengthen, settle *you*."

I am still a work in progress as many of us are currently today. We all remain righteous in the eyes of God, even when we are not acting or behaving our best. I know that he is in me as he is in you and because of this he is able to change the desires of our hearts.

Jehovah Chezeq – The Lord My Strength

My strength when I am weak

Isaiah 40:31 (Strength)

"But they that wait upon the LORD shall renew _their_ strength; they shall mount up with wings as eagles; they shall run, and not be weary; _and_ they shall walk, and not faint."

Philippians 4:13 (Strength)

"I can do all things through Christ which strengtheneth me."

Philippians 4:7 (Strength)

"And the peace of God, which passeth all understanding, shall keep your hearts and minds through Christ Jesus."

Psalms 18:32 (Strength)

"*It is* God that girdeth me with strength, and maketh my way perfect."

Philippians 2:13 (Strength)

"For it is God which worketh in you both to will and to do of *his* good pleasure."

Growing up in South Carolina gave me strength at an early age. I grew up working in the fields picking cotton, pulling weeds out of soy beans, sucking tobacco, cropping tobacco, handing tobacco and hanging tobacco in the barns. I worked in the fields from sunrise to sunset at a very young age. With God in me and with his strength, I understood the value on applying self in order to make a better future.

Jehovah Jireh – The Lord will Provide

Genesis 22:14

"And Abraham called the name of that place Jehovahjireh: as it is said *to* this day, In the mount of the LORD it shall be seen."

Psalms 54:4 (Provider)

"Behold, God *is* mine helper: the Lord *is* with them that uphold my soul."

Hebrews 13:5 (Provider)

"*Let your* conversation *be* without covetousness; *and be* content with such things as ye have: for he hath said, I will never leave thee, nor forsake thee."

Philippians 4:19 (Provider)

"But my God shall supply all your need according to his riches in glory by Christ Jesus."

John 16:13 (Provider)

"Howbeit when he, the Spirit of truth, is come, he will guide you into all truth: for he shall not speak of himself; but whatsoever he shall hear, *that* shall he speak: and he will shew you things to come."

When mother had surgery on her hand the Lord provided. Mother who was a presser at Hartsville Manufacturing could not press clothes due to the surgery leaving her out of work . Father worked on the farm but work was slow due to a brutal winter. He was not able to work as much making the money he did during summer. Our food began to get low on the verge of running out. Father had his pride but did not want to apply for food stamps. Mother who was a praying lady asked God to speak to father. God spoke, mother applied for food stamps which was approved. We were able to have food to sustain through the winter. God is good..

Jehovah Mephalti – The Lord My Deliverer

Psalms 18:2 (Deliverance)

"The LORD _is_ my rock, and my fortress, and my deliverer; my God, my strength, in whom I will trust; my buckler, and the horn of my salvation, _and_ my high tower."

Psalms 34:17 (Deliverance)

"_The righteous_ cry, and the LORD heareth, and delivereth them out of all their troubles."

Psalms 107:6 (Deliverance)

"Then they cried unto the LORD in their trouble, _and_ he delivered them out of their distresses."

2 Samuel 22:2 (Deliverance)

"And he said, The LORD *is* my rock, and my fortress, and my deliverer;"

Psalms 50:15 (Deliverance)

"And call upon me in the day of trouble: I will deliver thee, and thou shalt glorify me."

James 5:16 (Deliverance)

"Confess *your* faults one to another, and pray one for another, that ye may be healed. The effectual fervent prayer of a righteous man availeth much."

Psalms 34:4 (Deliverance)

"I sought the LORD, and he heard me, and delivered me from all my fears."

John 8:32 (Deliverance)

"And ye shall know the truth, and the truth shall make you free."

Romans 6:14 (Deliverance)

"For sin shall not have dominion over you: for ye are not under the law, but under grace."

John 15:7 (Deliverance)

"If ye abide in me, and my words abide in you, ye shall ask what ye will, and it shall be done unto you."

I have sinned and fallen short of his glory. A work in progress who prayed and confessed to God to make me better. I understood and appreciate what my elders were saying to me; keep on living, just live a little longer. I've learned that I had to go through for self, reach a point in my life where I needed to be delivered spiritually, mentally, financially, and emotionally as I went through my trials and tribulations.

Jehovah Rohi – The Lord My Shepherd

Psalms 23:1-6 (Shepherd)

"(A Psalm of David.) The LORD *is* my shepherd; I
shall not want."

Psalms 23:2 (Shepherd)

"He maketh me to lie down in green pastures: he
leadeth me beside the still waters."

Psalms 23:3 (Shepherd)

"He restoreth my soul: he leadeth me in the paths of
righteousness for his name's sake."

Psalms 23:4 (Shepherd)

"Yea, though I walk through the valley of the shadow of death, I will fear no evil: for thou *art* with me; thy rod and thy staff they comfort me."

Psalms 23:5 (Shepherd)

"Thou preparest a table before me in the presence of mine enemies: thou anointest my head with oil; my cup runneth over."

The Lord knows me better than I know myself. I do know that he is in my heart at all times. I can call on him quietly when at work, riding in my car or at any hour of the day when I need him. I know he will always be there with me. He is my shepherd that never leaves me. He continues to guide me, keep me strong when I'm weak, guide me when I'm lost, a friend and keep me safe.

Jehovah Kabodhi – The Lord My Glory

1 Corinthians 10:31 (Glory)

"Whether therefore ye eat, or drink, or whatsoever ye do, do all to the glory of God."

Philippians 2:9-11 (Glory)

"Wherefore God also hath highly exalted him, and given him a name which is above every name:"

Philippians 2:10 (Glory)

"That at the name of Jesus every knee should bow, of _things_ in heaven, and _things_ in earth, and _things_ under the earth;"

Philippians 2:11 (Glory)

"And *that* every tongue should confess that Jesus Christ *is* Lord, to the glory of God the Father."

Romans 11:36 (Glory)

"For of him, and through him, and to him, *are* all things: to whom *be* glory for ever. Amen."

Psalms 23:6 (Glory)

"Surely goodness and mercy shall follow me all the days of my life: and I will dwell in the house of the LORD for ever."

Romans 3:23 (Glory)

"For all have sinned, and come short of the glory of God;"

Isaiah 60:1 (Glory)

"Arise, shine; for thy light is come, and the glory of the LORD is risen upon thee."

Psalms 72:19 (Glory)

"And blessed *be* his glorious name for ever: and let the whole earth be filled *with* his glory; Amen, and Amen."

Matthew 5:16 (Glory)

"Let your light so shine before men, that they may see your good works, and glorify your Father which is in heaven

Jehovah Keren-Yish'i –
The Lord the Horn of My Salvation

John 3:16-17 (Salvation)

"For God so loved the world, that he gave his only begotten Son, that whosoever believeth in him should not perish, but have everlasting life."

John 3:17 (Salvation)

"For God sent not his Son into the world to condemn the world; but that the world through him might be saved."

Ephesians 2:8-9 (Salvation)

"For by grace are ye saved through faith; and that not of yourselves: _it is_ the gift of God:"

Ephesians 2:9 (Salvation)

"Not of works, lest any man should boast."

Romans 5:8 (Salvation)

"But God commendeth his love toward us, in that, while we were yet sinners, Christ died for us."

Isaiah 55:6-7 (Salvation)

"Seek ye the LORD while he may be found, call ye upon him while he is near:"

Isaiah 55:7 (Salvation)

"Let the wicked forsake his way, and the unrighteous man his thoughts: and let him return unto the LORD, and he will have mercy upon him; and to our God, for he will abundantly pardon

Romans 10:11-13 (Salvation)

"For the scripture saith, Whosoever believeth on him shall not be ashamed."

Romans 10:12 (Salvation)

"For there is no difference between the Jew and the Greek: for the same Lord over all is rich unto all that call upon him."

Romans 10:13 (Salvation)

"For whosoever shall call upon the name of the Lord shall be saved."

Matthew 7:21 (Salvation)

"Not every one that saith unto me, Lord, Lord, shall enter into the kingdom of heaven; but he that doeth the will of my Father which is in heaven."

Acts 2:38 (Salvation)

"Then Peter said unto them, Repent, and be baptized every one of you in the name of Jesus Christ for the remission of sins, and ye shall receive the gift of the Holy Ghost."

GRACE

Isaiah 40:31 (Grace)

"But they that wait upon the LORD shall renew *their* strength; they shall mount up with wings as eagles; they shall run, and not be weary; *and* they shall walk, and not faint."

2 Corinthians 12:9 (Grace)

"And he said unto me, My grace is sufficient for thee: for my strength is made perfect in weakness. Most gladly therefore will I rather glory in my infirmities, that the power of Christ may rest upon me."

Ephesians 2:8-9 (Grace)

"For by grace are ye saved through faith; and that not of yourselves: *it is* the gift of God:"

Ephesians 2:9 (Grace)

"Not of works, lest any man should boast."

Romans 6:14 (Grace)

"For sin shall not have dominion over you: for ye are not under the law, but under grace."

James 4:6 (Grace)

"But he giveth more grace. Wherefore he saith, God resisteth the proud, but giveth grace unto the humble."

1 Corinthians 15:10 (Grace)

"But by the grace of God I am what I am: and his grace which *was bestowed* upon me was not in vain; but I laboured more abundantly than they all: yet not I, but the grace of God which was with me."

Hebrews 4:16 (Grace)

"Let us therefore come boldly unto the throne of grace, that we may obtain mercy, and find grace to help in time of need."

1 Peter 5:10 (Grace)

"But the God of all grace, who hath called us unto his eternal glory by Christ Jesus, after that ye have suffered a while, make you perfect, stablish, strengthen, settle *you*."

If it were not by the grace of God, I could have been dead sleeping in my grave after my car accident. I returned home from being out at sea aboard my ship in Charleston. I caught a ride with a shipmate to Darlington to pickup my car from my parents home. I was out with a friend late in the morning hours when I felled asleep at the wheel of my car. I hit two street light poles totaling my car at 2:00am. It was grace that saved me. I did not have any broken bones but was in the hospital for a few day. I was able to leave later when mother told me the transmission was in the front seat next to me. It was God's grace that protected me.

POEM

By: Cornelious Coe

WHEN I

Only I know what I've been through
My friends don't know
Lord I only told you
I had hard times never gave up the faith
I put my trust in you
Never doubted your grace
When I was down you picked me up
When I was lost you came at no cost
When I was sick You made me well
In a world of sin you still took me in
I see the light you put before me
It was shining real bright so I can see
I'm a little weary trying to find my way
I just might stumble
I know I will make it one day, because
When I was down you picked me up
When I was lost you came at no cost
When I was sick you made me well
In a world of sin
You still took me in

FAITH

Hebrews 11:1 (Faith)

"Now faith is the substance of things hoped for, the evidence of things not seen."

2 Corinthians 5:7 (Faith)

"(For we walk by faith, not by sight:)"

Luke 1:37 (Faith)

"For with God nothing shall be impossible."

James 2:19 (Faith)

"Thou believest that there is one God; thou doest well: the devils also believe, and tremble."

Hebrews 11:6 (Faith)

"But without faith *it is* impossible to please *him*: for he that cometh to God must believe that he is, and *that* he is a rewarder of them that diligently seek him."

Matthew 21:22 (Faith)

"And all things, whatsoever ye shall ask in prayer, believing, ye shall receive."

Psalms 46:10 (Faith)

"Be still, and know that I *am* God: I will be exalted among the heathen, I will be exalted in the earth."

Proverbs 3:5-6 (Faith)

"Trust in the LORD with all thine heart; and lean not unto thine own understanding."

Proverbs 3:6 (Faith)

"In all thy ways acknowledge him, and he shall direct thy paths."

Romans 10:17 (Faith)

"So then faith *cometh* by hearing, and hearing by the word of God."

Luke 17:6

"And the Lord said, If ye had faith as a grain of mustard seed, ye might say unto this sycamine tree, Be thou plucked up by the root, and be thou planted in the sea; and it should obey you."

Mother always said "with faith you can accomplish anything". I would not be anything without faith. I trust in God and his word as he has never forsaken me. Faith allowed me to trust in his word to write this book. Faith has kept me strong when I was weak, faith kept me focus when I felt like giving up and giving in.

MERCY

1 John 1:9 (Mercy)

"If we confess our sins, he is faithful and just to forgive us *our* sins, and to cleanse us from all unrighteousness."

Matthew 5:7 (Mercy)

"Blessed *are* the merciful: for they shall obtain mercy."

Hebrews 4:16 (Mercy)

"Let us therefore come boldly unto the throne of grace, that we may obtain mercy, and find grace to help in time of need."

Colossians 3:12 (Mercy)

"Put on therefore, as the elect of God, holy and beloved, bowels of mercies, kindness, humbleness of mind, meekness, longsuffering;"

Luke 6:37 (Mercy)

"Judge not, and ye shall not be judged: condemn not, and ye shall not be condemned: forgive, and ye shall be forgiven:"

Micah 6:8 (Mercy)

"He hath shewed thee, O man, what *is* good; and what doth the LORD require of thee, but to do justly, and to love mercy, and to walk humbly with thy God"

Forgiveness

Ephesians 4:32 (Forgiveness)

"And be ye kind one to another, tenderhearted, forgiving one another, even as God for Christ's sake hath forgiven you."

Mark 11:25 (Forgiveness)

"And when ye stand praying, forgive, if ye have ought against any: that your Father also which is in heaven may forgive you your trespasses."

1 John 1:9 (Forgiveness)

"If we confess our sins, he is faithful and just to forgive us _our_ sins, and to cleanse us from all unrighteousness."

Matthew 6:14-15 (Forgiveness)

"For if ye forgive men their trespasses, your heavenly Father will also forgive you:"

Matthew 6:15 (Forgiveness)

"But if ye forgive not men their trespasses, neither will your Father forgive your trespasses."

Luke 6:27 (Forgiveness)

"But I say unto you which hear, Love your enemies, do good to them which hate you,"

Colossians 3:13 (Forgiveness)

"Forbearing one another, and forgiving one another, if any man have a quarrel against any: even as Christ forgave you, so also *do* ye."

Hope

Romans 12:12 (Hope)

"Rejoicing in hope; patient in tribulation; continuing instant in prayer;"

Romans 15:13 (Hope)

"Now the God of hope fill you with all joy and peace in believing, that ye may abound in hope, through the power of the Holy Ghost."

Deuteronomy 31:6 (Hope)

"Be strong and of a good courage, fear not, nor be afraid of them: for the LORD thy God, he _it is_ that doth go with thee; he will not fail thee, nor forsake thee."

Romans 5:2-5 (Hope)

"By whom also we have access by faith into this grace wherein we stand, and rejoice in hope of the glory of God."

Romans 5:3 (Hope)

"And not only *so*, but we glory in tribulations also: knowing that tribulation worketh patience;"

Romans 5:4 (Hope)

"And patience, experience; and experience, hope:"

Romans 5:5 (Hope)

"And hope maketh not ashamed; because the love of God is shed abroad in our hearts by the Holy Ghost which is given unto us."

Psalms 39:7 (Hope)

"And now, Lord, what wait I for? my hope *is* in thee."

Mark 9:23 (Hope)

"Jesus said unto him, If thou canst believe, all things *are* possible to him that believeth."

Romans 8:24-25 (Hope)

"For we are saved by hope: but hope that is seen is not hope: for what a man seeth, why doth he yet hope for?"

Romans 8:25 (Hope)

"But if we hope for that we see not, *then* do we with patience wait for *it*."

Psalms 71:14 (Hope)

"But I will hope continually, and will yet praise thee more and more."

VICTORY

Deuteronomy 20: (Victory)

"For the LORD your God *is* he that goeth with you, to fight for you against your enemies, to save you."

Psalms 108:13 (Victory)

"Through God we shall do valiantly: for he *it is that* shall tread down our enemies."

Ephesians 6:13 (Victory)

"Wherefore take unto you the whole armour of God, that ye may be able to withstand in the evil day, and having done all, to stand."

Ephesians 6:10 (Victory)

"Finally, my brethren, be strong in the Lord, and in the power of his might."

1 Corinthians 15:57 (Victory)

"But thanks *be* to God, which giveth us the victory through our Lord Jesus Christ."

Romans 8:37 (Victory)

"Nay, in all these things we are more than conquerors through him that loved us."

2 Corinthians 2:14 (Victory)

"Now thanks *be* unto God, which always causeth us to triumph in Christ, and maketh manifest the savour of his knowledge by us in every place."

Romans 8:31 (Victory)

"What shall we then say to these things? If God *be* for us, who *can be* against us?"

Romans 8:39 (Victory)

"Nor height, nor depth, nor any other creature, shall be able to separate us from the love of God, which is in Christ Jesus our Lord."

REJOICE

Psalms 118:24 (Rejoice)

"This *is* the day *which* the LORD hath made; we will rejoice and be glad in it."

Psalms 107:1 (Rejoice)

"O give thanks unto the LORD, for *he is* good: for his mercy *endureth* for ever."

Philippians 4:4 (Rejoice)

"Rejoice in the Lord alway: *and* again I say, Rejoice."

Psalms 5:11 (Rejoice)

"But let all those that put their trust in thee rejoice: let them ever shout for joy, because thou defendest them: let them also that love thy name be joyful in thee."

1 John 4:18 (Rejoice)

"There is no fear in love; but perfect love casteth out fear: because fear hath torment. He that feareth is not made perfect in love."

Psalms 91:1-2 (Rejoice)

"He that dwelleth in the secret place of the most High shall abide under the shadow of the Almighty."

Psalms 91:2 (Rejoice)

"I will say of the LORD, *He is* my refuge and my fortress: my God; in him will I trust."

Gratitude

Matthew 6:21 (Gratitude)

"For where your treasure is, there will your heart be also."

Ephesians 5:20 (Gratitude)

"Giving thanks always for all things unto God and the Father in the name of our Lord Jesus Christ;"

Romans 8:28 (Gratitude)

"And we know that all things work together for good to them that love God, to them who are the called according to *his* purpose."

Psalms 100:1 (Gratitude)

"(A Psalm of praise.) Make a joyful noise unto the LORD, all ye lands."

Psalms 100:2 (Gratitude)

"Serve the LORD with gladness: come before his presence with singing."

Psalms 100:3 (Gratitude)

"Know ye that the LORD he *is* God: *it is* he *that* hath made us, and not we ourselves; *we are* his people, and the sheep of his pasture."

Psalms 100:4 (Gratitude)

"Enter into his gates with thanksgiving, *and* into his courts with praise: be thankful unto him, *and* bless his name."

Psalms 100:5 (Gratitude)

"For the LORD *is* good; his mercy *is* everlasting; and his truth *endureth* to all generations."

Colossians 3:15 (Gratitude)

"And let the peace of God rule in your hearts, to the which also ye are called in one body; and be ye thankful."

Colossians 3:16 (Gratitude)

"Let the word of Christ dwell in you richly in all wisdom; teaching and admonishing one another in psalms and hymns and spiritual songs, singing with grace in your hearts to the Lord."

Colossians 3:17 (Gratitude)

"And whatsoever ye do in word or deed, *do* all in the name of the Lord Jesus, giving thanks to God and the Father by him."

Never Give Up

Galatians 6:9 (Never Give Up)

"And let us not be weary in well doing: for in due season we shall reap, if we faint not."

2 Chronicles 15:7 (Never Give Up)

"Be ye strong therefore, and let not your hands be weak: for your work shall be rewarded."

Matthew 19:26 (Never Give Up)

"But Jesus beheld _them_, and said unto them, With men this is impossible; but with God all things are possible."

John 8:12 (Never Give Up)

"Then spake Jesus again unto them, saying, I am the light of the world: he that followeth me shall not walk in darkness, but shall have the light of life."

Giving up was not an option in my life. If I gave up, I could not improve my life. I could not make life better for my family. I would not know what doors would open for me by giving up. Yes, life has not been easy but I realized that God had a plan for me, and continues to have a plan for me.

Prayer

Philippians 4:6 (Prayer)

"Be careful for nothing; but in every thing by prayer and supplication with thanksgiving let your requests be made known unto God

Mark 11:24 (Prayer)

"Therefore I say unto you, What things soever ye desire, when ye pray, believe that ye receive _them_, and ye shall have _them_."

1 Thessalonians 5:17 (Prayer)

"Pray without ceasing."

Luke 11:9 (Prayer)

"And I say unto you, Ask, and it shall be given you; seek, and ye shall find; knock, and it shall be opened unto you."

Matthew 6:6 (Prayer)

"But thou, when thou prayest, enter into thy closet, and when thou hast shut thy door, pray to thy Father which is in secret; and thy Father which seeth in secret shall reward thee openly."

James 5:16 (Prayer)

"Confess *your* faults one to another, and pray one for another, that ye may be healed. The effectual fervent prayer of a righteous man availeth much."

Psalms 34:17 (Prayer)

"*The righteous* cry, and the LORD heareth, and delivereth them out of all their troubles."

Prosperity

Deuteronomy 8:18 (Prosperity)

"But thou shalt remember the LORD thy God: for _it is_ he that giveth thee power to get wealth, that he may establish his covenant which he sware unto thy fathers, as _it is_ this day."

Philippians 4:19 (Prosperity)

"But my God shall supply all your need according to his riches in glory by Christ Jesus."

2 Corinthians 9:8 (Prosperity)

"And God _is_ able to make all grace abound toward you; that ye, always having all sufficiency in all _things_, may abound to every good work:"

Malachi 3:10 (Prosperity)

"Bring ye all the tithes into the storehouse, that there may be meat in mine house, and prove me now herewith, saith the LORD of hosts, if I will not open you the windows of heaven, and pour you out a blessing, that *there shall* not *be room* enough *to receive it*."

2 Corinthians 8:9 (Prosperity)

"For ye know the grace of our Lord Jesus Christ, that, though he was rich, yet for your sakes he became poor, that ye through his poverty might be rich."

Luke 6:38 (Prosperity)

"Give, and it shall be given unto you; good measure, pressed down, and shaken together, and running over, shall men give into your bosom. For with the same measure that ye mete withal it shall be measured to you again."

Favor

Psalms 5:12

"For thou, LORD, wilt bless the righteous; with favour wilt thou compass him as *with* a shield."

Psalms 84:11

"For the LORD God *is* a sun and shield: the LORD will give grace and glory: no good *thing* will he withhold from them that walk uprightly

Psalms 75:6

"For promotion *cometh* neither from the east, nor from the west, nor from the south."

Psalms 75:7

"But God *is* the judge: he putteth down one, and setteth up another."

God Has Smiled on Me (God Will Supply)

In my closing, I want to leave with saying God has Smiled on Me and He will Smile on You. He has supplied everything that I need and will supply everything you need. I'm speaking from what I've been through in life. I did not grow up with much as a young child but he supplied me with a loving mother and father. Some days it did not seem we were going to make it but we did with the help of family and by God's Grace and Mercy. I did not always have the best clothes on my back or shoes on my feet but he supplied the very best that my parents could buy. My sisters did not have the store bought dresses but he supplied mother with a sewing machine and the skills to make women clothing. We did not have a fancy car to drive but he did supply father and mother with a car to get back and forth to work. My sisters and I did not have summer off but he did supply us with good health to work in the fields so we could help the family.. Later in life when I could not see my way I got on my knees and prayed. God answer prayers. I had to trust in him and trust his word. He has been good to me when I was not good to myself. I had to learn the hard way that I could not do it alone. Yes, hard headed thinking I had all the answers but quickly found out that I had to ask the Lord in prayer to guide me to help fight my battles. When I look back over my life, I see all of the things the Lord has done for me. I also see all the things he showed to me that I did not obey. He kept me in my right mind mentally. He has been my counselor when emotionally exhausted due to the death of my father and my cousin who was a brother to me, with my job and life. I talked to friends but when I gave it to the Lord he helped me to get through the pain. I could talk to God at the gym, in my car, at work or in my house. When I needed to cry, he was there and did not judge, instead his spirit was a comfort to me. As James Cleveland wrote "God has smiled on me, He has set me free. God has Smiled on me, He's been good to me. He is the source of all my joy, He fills me with His

Love, everything that I need. He sends it down from above". God continues to smile on me and supply. He speaks to my spirit, helping me to continue to grow spiritually as I trust in his word. I believed in my gifts, talents and do the very best for my family and friends. As you continue to read, believe and trust that God Smiles on you. He will supply no matter where you are in your life. Do not let the burdens that you carry keep you down and depressed. You must continue to call on the Lord in prayer. Never give up but know and believe your victory is around the corner. Keep your faith because you can do all things through Christ which strengtheneth you. Forgive those have hurt you and know that Jesus Lives in You no matter where you are in life or where you go in life.

CoeBooksPublishing

THANK YOU FOR BUYING
A CORNELIOUS COE BOOK.
IF YOU ENJOYED THIS
TITLE, YOU MIGHT WANT
TO CHECK OUT OTHER
BOOKS IN OUR CATALOG.

Contact Information: CoeBooksPublishing@yahoo.com

Website: coebookspublish1.godaddysites.com

WHAT DOESN'T KILL YOU CAN ONLY MAKE YOU STRONGER
2012, by Cornelious Coe
An old saying emphasizing the importance of not giving up or giving in to circumstance. Life does not always go as planned. One must have faith, believe in self and have a strong support system with family and friends. One must remain positive, stay strong no matter what challenges, obstacles, or hurdles you must go around, under or over.
237 pages. Paperback.

REFLECTIONS
2013 by Cornelious Coe
Music CD: A collection of poems to song about life, love, and relationship. You can read the poems included in Reflections book of poems then listen to each recorded song.

Live
In
Me
Jesus
Uplifting Scriptures

Cornelious Coe

LIVE IN ME JESUS (UPLIFTING SCRIPTURES)

Made in the USA
Columbia, SC
20 April 2019